MW00997632

Frontispiece. 1. Whip snake. 2–3. Colubrine snakes. {TOMUS II, TABULA 33}

Seba's Snakes
and Lizards

240 Illustrations

Albertus Seba

Dover Publications, Inc., Mineola, New York

Publisher's Note

An avid collector of curiosities, Albertus Seba, an Amsterdam pharmacist, compiled a stunning visual record of thousands of animal specimens in his rare, four-volume *Locupletissimi Rerum Naturalium Thesauri Accurata Descriptio* (1734–1765). In 1731, Seba had commissioned a host of artists and engravers to assist him in this massive undertaking. His unprecedented display of scientifically precise drawings reveals the tremendous pride he took in his vast collection and in the wondrous diversity of nature. His unique assortment of natural specimens remains a testament to his dedication and passion for collecting miscellany.

The present volume reproduces, in full color, a selection of sixty plates from Seba's pioneering, eighteenth-century work. The magnificent hand-colored prints that appear here depict a wide variety of snakes, lizards, and other reptiles. This new compilation of exotic illustrations, carefully selected from one of the most treasured catalogs of all time, will enthrall artists and students fascinated by herpetology.

Bibliographical Note

This Dover edition, first published in 2006, is a new selection of 60 plates from *Locupletissimi Rerum Naturalium Thesauri Accurata Descriptio* by Albertus Seba, originally published as a four-volume set in Amsterdam between 1734 and 1765. All animal and plant identifications included here are based on Seba's research. The Publisher's Note has been specially written for the present edition.

DOVER *Pictorial Archive* SERIES

This book belongs to the Dover Pictorial Archive Series. You may use the designs and illustrations for graphics and crafts applications, free and without special permission, provided that you include no more than ten in the same publication or project. (For permission for additional use, please write to Permissions Department, Dover Publications, Inc., 31 East 2nd Street, Mineola, N.Y. 11501.)

However, republication or reproduction of any illustration by any other graphic service, whether it be in a book or in any other design resource, is strictly prohibited.

Library of Congress Cataloging-in-Publication Data

Seba, Albertus, 1665–1736.
   [Locupletissimi rerum naturalium thesauri. Selections]
   Seba's snakes and lizards : 240 illustrations / Albertus Seba.
      p. cm. — (Dover pictorial archive series)
   ISBN 0-486-45368-5 (pbk.)
     1. Snakes—Pictorial works. 2. Lizards—Pictorial works. 3. Seba, Albertus, 1665–1736.
Locupletissimi rerum naturalium thesauri. I. Title. II. Series.

QL666.O6S3918 2006
597.9022'2—dc22

                                         2006046336

Manufactured in the United States of America
Dover Publications, Inc., 31 East 2nd Street, Mineola, N.Y. 11501

PLATE 1. 1–2. Lizards. 3. Snake from Guinea. 4–5. Chameleons. [TOMUS I, TABULA 83]

Fig. 1

Fig. 5

Fig. 3

Fig. 4

Fig. 2

PLATE 2. 1–2. Iguanas or anoles. 3. Lizard. 4–5. Newts. [TOMUS I, TABULA 89]

Fig. 1

Fig. 2

Fig. 3

Fig. 4

Fig. 5

PLATE 3. 1–4. Lizards. 5. Snake from Brazil. [TOMUS I, TABULA 91]

PLATE 4. 1–5. Lizards and anoles. [TOMUS I, TABULA 92]

Fig. 1

Fig. 2

Fig. 3

Fig. 4

Fig. 5

Fig. 6

Fig. 2

Fig. 4

Fig. 1

Fig. 3

Fig. 5

PLATE 5. 1–4. Lizards. [TOMUS I, TABULA 93]

Fig. 1

Fig. 3

Fig. 5

Fig. 2

Fig. 4

PLATE 6. 1–2. Green iguanas. 3–4. Agamas. [TOMUS I, TABULA 95]

Fig. 1

Fig. 2

Fig. 3

Fig. 4

Fig. 5

Fig. 6

PLATE 7. 1–3. Common tegus. 4–6. Lizards. [TOMUS I, TABULA 96]

Fig. 3

Fig. 5

Fig. 1

Fig. 2

Fig. 4

PLATE 8. 1–5. Squamata from South America. 3. Green iguana. [TOMUS I, TABULA 97]

Fig. 1

Fig. 2

Fig. 3

PLATE 9. 1. Green iguana. 2. Polychrotidae. 3. Common tegu. [TOMUS I, TABULA 98]

PLATE 10. 1. Common tegu. 2. Monitor from South East Asia. 3. Snake from Madeira. 4. Hummingbird. [TOMUS I, TABULA 99]

Fig. 1

Fig. 2

Fig. 3

Fig. 4

PLATE 11. 1. Common basilisk. 2–3. Squamata. 4–5. Snakes from Ceylon. [TOMUS I, TABULA 100]

Fig. 1

PLATE 12. 1. Squamata. [TOMUS I, TABULA 101]

Fig. 6

Fig. 7

Fig. 2

Fig. 3

Fig. 4

Fig. 1

Fig. 5

PLATE 13. 1–5. Crocodiles. [TOMUS I, TABULA 103]

Fig. 1

Fig. 2

PLATE 14. 1. Crocodile. 2. Lizard. [TOMUS I, TABULA 106]

Fig. 1

Fig. 2

Fig. 3

PLATE 15. 1–3. Iguanas. [TOMUS I, TABULA 107]

PLATE 16. 1–3. Snakes. 4. Caterpillar. 5–6. Lizards. 7–10. Heath family. [TOMUS II, TABULA 9]

PLATE 17. 1–2. Western shovelnose snake. 3. Snake from America.
4. Scorpion eater/Scorpion-eating snake. 9. Spring heath. [TOMUS II, TABULA 11]

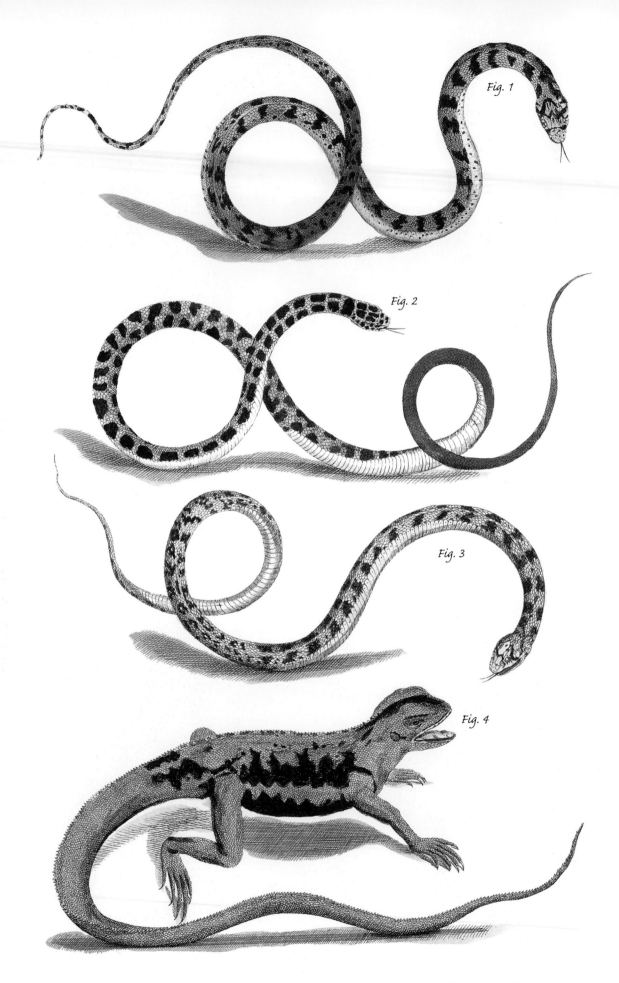

Fig. 1

Fig. 2

Fig. 3

Fig. 4

PLATE 18. 1–3. Snakes from America and Ambon. 4. Agama. [TOMUS II, TABULA 14]

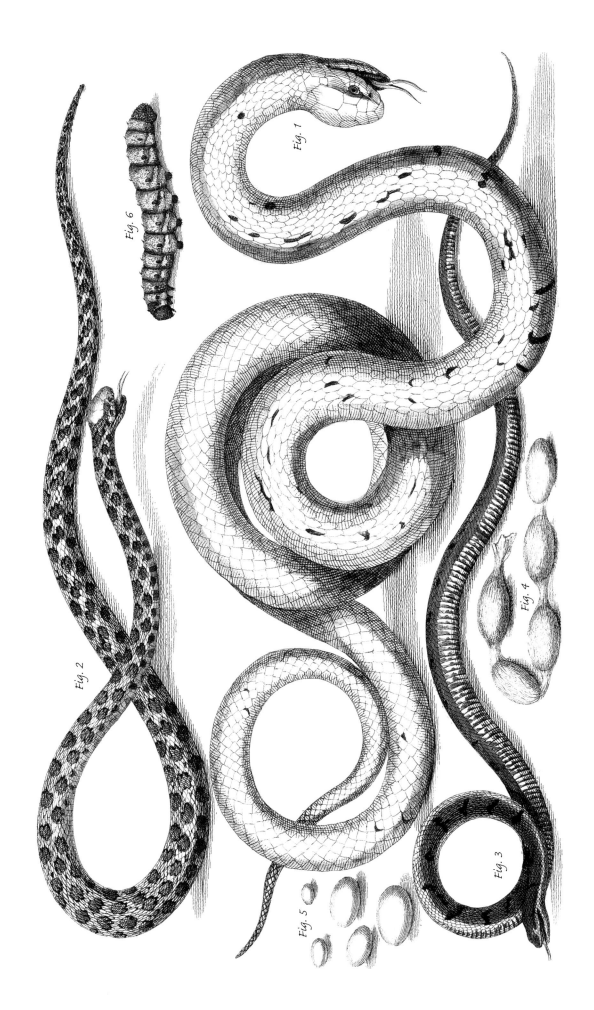

PLATE 19. 1. Southwestern grass snake. 2. Snake from Ambon.
3. Snake from America. 4–5. Eggs of a snake. 6. Caterpillar. [TOMUS II, TABULA 15]

Fig. 1

Fig. 2

Fig. 3

Fig. 4

Fig. 5

Fig. 6

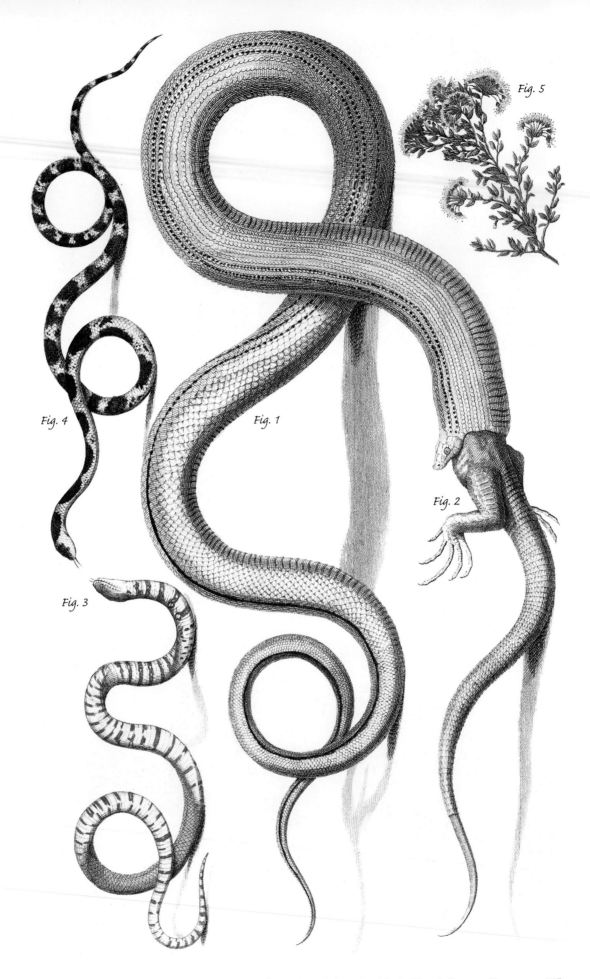

PLATE 20. 1, 3–4. Snakes from Ambon (1), Africa (3), and America (4). 2. Lizard. [TOMUS II, TABULA 17]

PLATE 21. 1–4. Snakes from various regions. 2. Sand boa. [TOMUS II, TABULA 18]

Fig. 1

Fig. 2

Fig. 3

PLATE 22. 1. Snake from Nova Hispania. 2–3. Snakes from different continents. [TOMUS II, TABULA 26]

Fig. 1

Fig. 2

Fig. 3

Fig. 4

Fig. 5

Fig. 6

PLATE 23. 1. Boid snake. 2–5. Snakes from different continents. 6. Lizard or Agama. [TOMUS II, TABULA 27]

PLATE 24. 1–6. Snakes from South America. [TOMUS II, TABULA 28]

Fig. 3

Fig. 2

Fig. 1

PLATE 25. 1. Anaconda. 2. Mouse. 3. American ratsnake. [TOMUS II, TABULA 29]

Fig. 3

Fig. 1

Fig. 2

Fig. 4

PLATE 26. 1. Snake from Ambon. 2. Lizard. 3. Snake from America. 4. Orchid family. [TOMUS II, TABULA 30]

PLATE 27. 1–5. Snakes from Siam. 6–7. Heath family. [TOMUS II, TABULA 34]

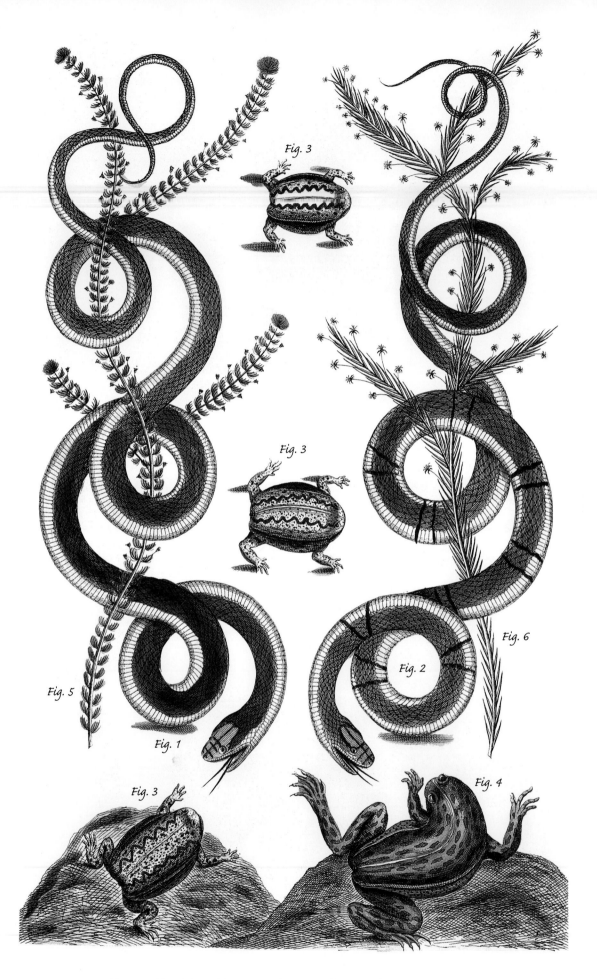

Fig. 3

Fig. 3

Fig. 5

Fig. 1

Fig. 6

Fig. 2

Fig. 3

Fig. 4

PLATE 28. 1–2. Snakes from Africa. 3. Narrow-mouthed toad. 4. Frog. [TOMUS II, TABULA 37]

PLATE 29. 1. Bird from America. 2–4. Various snakes. 6. Sunflower family. [TOMUS II, TABULA 40]

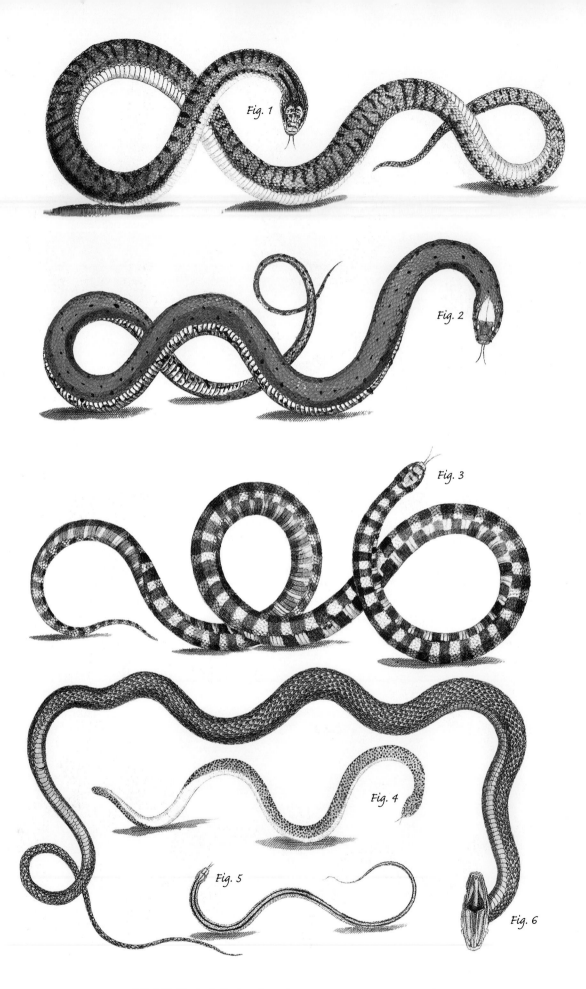

PLATE 30. 1–6. Snakes from America. [TOMUS II, TABULA 42]

Fig. 1

Fig. 2

Fig. 5

Fig. 6

Fig. 3

Fig. 4

PLATE 31. 1–2. Snakes from America. 3–4. Snakes from Africa. 5–6. Everlasting flower. [TOMUS II, TABULA 43]

Fig. 1

Fig. 2

Fig. 3

Fig. 4

PLATE 32. 1–4. Snakes from different continents. {TOMUS II, TABULA 46}

Fig. 3

Fig. 2

Fig. 1

PLATE 33. 1. Grass snake. 2. Giant anteater (young). 3. Tree groundsel and long-horned beetle. [TOMUS II, TABULA 47]

Fig. 2

Fig. 1

Fig. 3

Fig. 4

PLATE 34. 1. Grass snake and long-horned beetle.
2. Snake from Ceylon. 3. Pistache. 4. Milk vetch. [TOMUS II, TABULA 48]

Fig. 3

Fig. 2

Fig. 1

PLATE 35. 1. Garden boa. 2. Unidentified. 3. Australian blackwood family. [TOMUS II, TABULA 50]

Fig. 1

Fig. 2

Fig. 3

Fig. 4

PLATE 36. 1–3. Snakes from Java (1), Martinique (2), and Cuba (3).
4. Asian longnose whipsnake. [TOMUS II, TABULA 53]

PLATE 37. 1–2. Snakes from Ambon. 3–4. Snakes from Africa. [TOMUS II, TABULA 54]

Fig. 1

Fig. 2

Fig. 3

Fig. 4

PLATE 38. 1–2, 4. Snakes from Ceylon. 3. Nose-horned viper. [TOMUS II, TABULA 55]

Fig. 1

Fig. 3

Fig. 2

PLATE 39. 1–3. Various snakes. [TOMUS II, TABULA 57]

Fig. 2

Fig. 1

Fig. 3

PLATE 40. 1. Snake from Asia. 2. Snake from Guadeloupe. 3. Snake from Japan. {TOMUS II, TABULA 58}

PLATE 41. 1–4. Various snakes. [TOMUS II, TABULA 60]

PLATE 42. 1. Snake from St. Cruz. 2–6. Snakes from America. 7–9. Maidenhair fern. [TOMUS II, TABULA 64]

Fig. 2

Fig. 6

Fig. 4

Fig. 3

Fig. 1

Fig. 5

PLATE 43. 1–4. Snakes from America. 5–6. Sunflower family. [TOMUS II, TABULA 66]

PLATE 44. 1–3. Snakes from America. 4–5. Unidentified. 6–7. Pea family. [TOMUS II, TABULA 71]

PLATE 45. 1. Pine snake/Bull snake. 2. Snake from Brazil. 3–4. Ringed lizards. [TOMUS II, TABULA 73]

PLATE 46. 1. Garden tree boa. [TOMUS II, TABULA 74]

Fig. 3

Fig. 1

Fig. 5

Fig. 2

Fig. 4

PLATE 47. 1–5. Snakes from America. [TOMUS II, TABULA 75]

Fig. 1

Fig. 2

Fig. 3

Fig. 4

Fig. 5

PLATE 48. 1. Bushmaster. 2–3. Snakes from Ceylon. 4–5. Lizards. [TOMUS II, TABULA 76]

PLATE 49. 1. Emerald tree boa. [TOMUS II, TABULA 81]

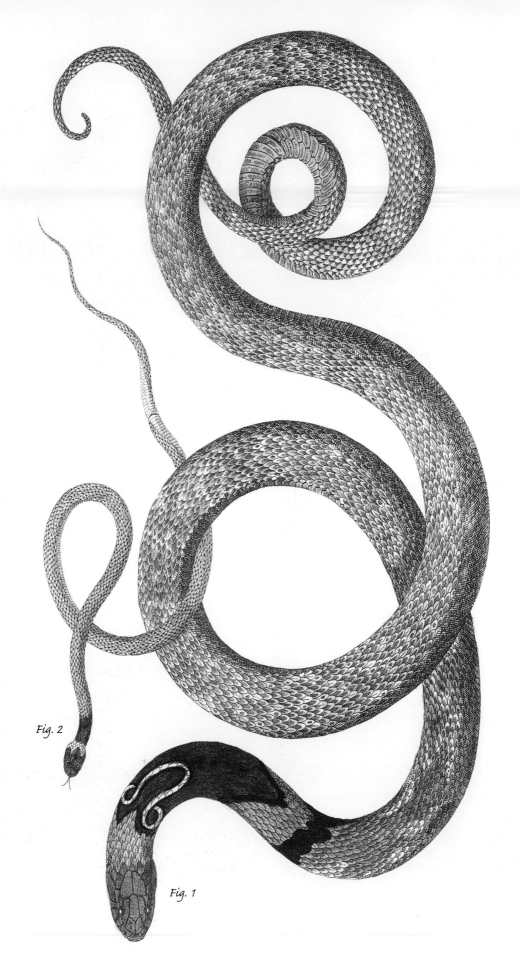

Fig. 2

Fig. 1

PLATE 50. 1. Common cobra. 2. Snake from Peru. [TOMUS II, TABULA 85]

Fig. 3

Fig. 1

Fig. 2

Fig. 3

PLATE 51. 1. Snake from Brazil. 2. Black-crested tyrant. 3. Unidentified. [TOMUS II, TABULA 87]

PLATE 52. 1. Rainbow boa. 2. Snake from Ceylon. [TOMUS II, TABULA 88]

PLATE 53. 1. Boid snake. [TOMUS II, TABULA 91]

PLATE 54. 1. Common boa. [TOMUS II, TABULA 92]

Fig. 1

Fig. 2

PLATE 55. 1. Poisonous snake. 2. Unidentified. [TOMUS II, TABULA 93]

PLATE 56. 1. Rainbow boa. [TOMUS II, TABULA 98]

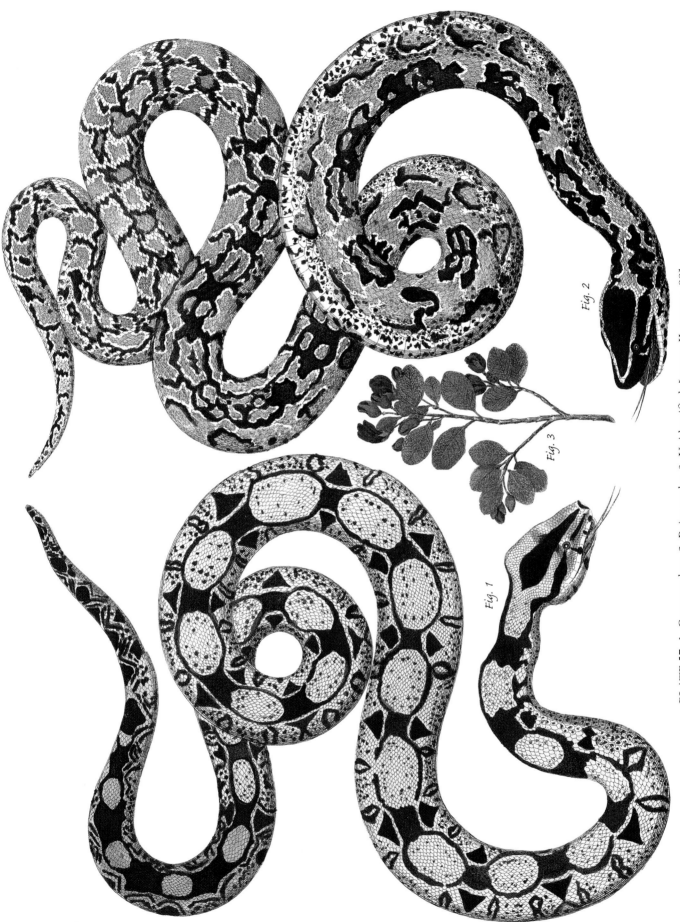

PLATE 57. 1. Common boa. 2. Boine snake. 3. Unidentified. [TOMUS II, TABULA 99]

Fig. 1

Fig. 2

Fig. 3

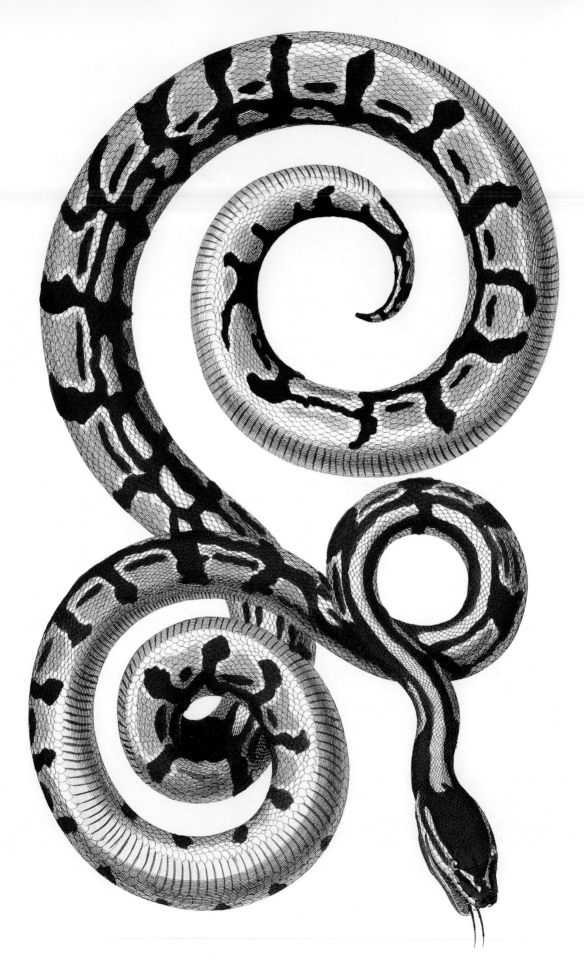

PLATE 58. 1. Royal python. {TOMUS II, TABULA 102}

PLATE 59. 1. Reticulated python. [TOMUS II, TABULA 104]